Forgiveness is the key to freedom

How letting go of the past opens the door to inner peace and lasting joy

By
Pastor Henry Owens Jr

Table Of Content

Dedication

I want to dedicate this book to My Lord and Savior, Jesus Christ.

Also, I would like to dedicate this book to my wife, Latrice L Owens. Thank you for all your encouragement and support.

To my daughters Tatiyanna L Owens and Brittany M Owens/Ellis.

To my seven granddaughters, who bring me so much joy.

Acknowledgment

I want to acknowledge my Lord and Savior, Jesus Christ. Without His Wisdom, none of this would have been possible.

My wife Latrice L Owens, my children Tatiyanna Owens and Brittany Ellis, and my seven granddaughters Amiyah Jackson, Layanna Ellis, A'sani Ellis, Serenity Ellis, Grace Ellis, Zyiah Ellis, and Zariah Matthews—love you!

My father and mother in the Gospel, Pastor Glenn & Gwen Taylor of Reno, NV, thank you for your encouragement over the years.

Elder Waterford of Los Angeles, CA, helped me obtain my ministry license.

Minister Bowers of Los Angeles, CA, encouraged me to preach the gospel in my youth.

My three sisters, Myrdle Broughton, Samantha Butler, and Patricia Owens, who has gone home to be with The Lord.

My mother, Clester Willis-Jefferson, who has gone on to be with The Lord, inspired me to evangelize the world with my auntie and her twin sister, Vester Moore.

My brothers in life are Lenard and Monique Dotson, Matthew and Rhonda Knight, Anthony and Loretta Velasquez, Vincent Stewart, Glenn Taylor II, Eddie Butler, Mitchell and Geishula Moore Jr., Terrell and Tara Taylor, and Tabu and Ebony McKnight.

About the Author

Pastor Henry Owens Jr. is a seasoned preacher, teacher, and servant of God who began his ministry journey at the young age of twelve when he was licensed to preach the gospel. From childhood, his passion for the Word of God set him apart as a student of Scripture and a voice of wisdom and revelation. For over forty years, Pastor Owens has faithfully served in multiple churches and ministries, teaching and preaching the transformative message of Christ with humility and power.

His lifelong study of the books of Daniel and Revelation has deepened his understanding of prophetic truth, spiritual discipline, and the grace of God. He is known for his practical teaching style—combining biblical insight, personal transparency, and Spirit-led revelation that brings Scripture to life.

Pastor Owens leads weekly Bible study sessions via YouTube and Facebook Live, where he and his wife, Latrice L. Owens, continue to minister to people around the world. Together, they have been married for more than 35 years, are blessed with two daughters, Tatiyanna L. Owens and Brittany M. Owens-Ellis, and are the proud grandparents of seven granddaughters—Amiyah, Layanna, A'sani, Serenity, Grace, Zyiah, and Zariah—each a precious reminder of God's generational faithfulness.

Pastor Owens' life and ministry are dedicated to spreading the message of forgiveness, restoration, and freedom through Christ, believing that when the heart truly forgives, heaven opens, healing begins, and chains are broken.

Book Synopsis

Forgiveness is the Key to Freedom: Unlocking the Power of Biblical Forgiveness is a spiritual guide that challenges believers to embrace forgiveness not as a choice, but as a divine command that leads to peace, healing, and freedom. In a world weighed down by bitterness, pain, and division, Pastor Henry Owens delivers a life-changing message grounded in Scripture and personal revelation: forgiveness is the spiritual key that unlocks heaven's blessings and restores the soul.

Through twelve biblically rich chapters, Pastor Owens takes readers on a journey of transformation—exploring forgiveness from God's perspective, exposing the dangers of unforgiveness, and revealing how mercy mirrors the very heart of Christ. Drawing from the words of Jesus, powerful parables, and modern examples, he shows that forgiveness is not about excusing sin, but about freeing the heart from bondage.

Readers will discover how unforgiveness blocks prayers and blessings, why forgiveness is tied to emotional and physical healing, and how prayer restores the heart toward reconciliation. Each chapter offers practical steps, biblical examples, and heartfelt encouragement to help readers break free from pain, release bitterness, and walk in obedience to God's Word.

At its core, Forgiveness is the Key to Freedom is a roadmap to spiritual liberty. It calls every reader to let go of the past, trust God with justice, and embrace the healing that only comes through Christ. In doing so, they will find what the world cannot offer: true peace, renewed joy, and the f

Foreword
By Shondra Sparks – Sutton

In a world where holding onto grudges and harboring resentment can seem easier than letting go, the message of forgiveness stands as a beacon of hope and healing. Forgiveness is a profound and transformative journey that touches the very core of our being. In " Forgiveness is the Key to Freedom: Unlocking The Power of Biblical Forgiveness ," Henry Owens masterfully guides us through the intricate and often challenging path of forgiveness. The author shares a unique perspective on the promises and commandments of God, revealing that forgiveness is not merely an option but a divine requirement.

Throughout this book, Owens demonstrates the commandments of God concerning forgiveness through the scriptures, offering a clearer understanding of the Word of God. He emphasizes that we do not have free will when it comes to forgiveness and obedience; these are mandates from God that we must embrace wholeheartedly.

In this book, Owens explores why forgiveness matters so much to God, how it impacts our spiritual realm, and the ultimate example of forgiveness demonstrated by Jesus on the cross. Owens writes through biblical teachings, personal anecdotes, and evidence by scripture the transformative power of forgiveness and how it can lead to a life of peace, joy, and spiritual freedom.

As you read "Forgiveness is the Key to Freedom," I encourage you to open your heart and mind to the possibility of forgiveness. The journey to forgiveness is not easy. The deep pain, betrayal, pride and desire for justice make it difficult to let go of offenses. Owens provides practical steps and spiritual insights to help readers overcome these obstacles and embrace forgiveness as a lifestyle. From understanding the difference between forgiveness and reconciliation recognizing their physical and emotional benefits of letting go, this book offers a roadmap to healing and restoration.

Now, let's be honest – forgiveness can be tough. It's like trying to eat just one potato chip or resisting the urge to hit the snooze button in the morning. But trust me, the rewards are worth it!

Owens, a dedicated Pastor and preacher of the Word of God, is more than qualified to deliver this powerful message. Throughout the book Owens demonstrates through the Word of God that if we do not forgive one another, our Father will not forgive our sins. As stated in *Matthew 6:14-15* – "For if you forgive other people when they sin against you, your heavenly Father will also forgive you. But if you do not forgive others their sins, your Father will not forgive your sins."

Throughout the book, Owens demonstrates through the Word of God, that forgiveness is a gift from God, that we must extend to others. Owens wraps this gift up beautifully, showing us, that forgiveness is the key to a rewarding relationship with Christ, by highlighting its eternal rewards, its ability to set us free, remove spiritual barriers, unlock doors closed by bitterness, bring healing to our body, mind, and spirit.

I am truly honored to have written a foreword for this book. Having personally benefited from Owens' teachings, I am a testament that this book will be a valuable contribution to others who believe in Christ. This book was not only inspired by Christ but was ordained by God. As you read this book, you will begin to understand that there is no free will, and we must forgive as Christ commands.

As you begin your journey of forgiveness by reading this book, I pray that you be transformed through the application of the Word of God, which is the foundation of the entire book that Owens has written so impeccably. So, grab a cup of coffee, find a cozy spot, and get ready to dive into a book that will not only make you self-reflect but also transform your life. May this book inspire you to embrace forgiveness as a lifestyle and experience the profound freedom and joy that comes wit

Title: Forgiveness is the Key to Freedom: Unlocking The Power of Biblical Forgiveness

Have you ever held onto a grudge so tightly that it seemed to consume your thoughts and emotions? Have you ever struggled to forgive someone, only to realize that the weight of bitterness was hurting you more than the one who wronged you? What if I told you that forgiveness is not just about setting someone else free—it's about setting yourself free?

Forgiveness is one of the most powerful spiritual keys given by God. It is not merely an act of kindness or a passive decision to "let things go." Forgiveness is a divine principle that unlocks the power of healing, restoration, and peace. It is the foundation of our relationship with God and with others.

Why Does Forgiveness Matter So Much to God?

📖 Matthew 6:14-15 – "For if you forgive other people when they sin against you, your heavenly Father will also forgive you. But if you do not forgive others their sins, your Father will not forgive your sins."

God takes forgiveness seriously because it reflects His character. He is a forgiving God, and He calls His children to reflect that same heart of mercy. When we hold onto unforgiveness, we are blocking His blessings and power from flowing into our lives. Unforgiveness is not just a personal issue—it is a spiritual roadblock.

The Power of Forgiveness in the Spiritual Realm

Every time you choose to forgive, something shifts in the spiritual realm. Forgiveness breaks strongholds, releases bondage, and opens the heavens over your life.

📖 Ephesians 4:32 – "Be kind and compassionate to one another, forgiving each other, just as in Christ God forgave you."

When we refuse to forgive, we align ourselves with the enemy's tactics. The devil thrives in division, bitterness, and resentment because these things separate us from God. However, when we choose to forgive, we step into God's divine protection and healing power.

Jesus, The Ultimate Example of Forgiveness

There is no greater display of forgiveness than Jesus on the cross. Even as He was being mocked, beaten, and nailed to a tree, He uttered these life-changing words:

📖 Luke 23:34 – "Father, forgive them, for they do not know what they are doing."

Jesus, in His final moments, showed us that forgiveness is not based on the worthiness of the offender—it is a gift of grace. If Jesus could forgive those who crucified Him, how much more should we extend forgiveness to those who hurt us?

Why Do People Struggle to Forgive?

If forgiveness is so powerful, why do many people find it so difficult? Here are some reasons:

1. **Deep Pain and Betrayal** – Some wounds cut so deeply that it feels impossible to forgive.
2. **Pride and Spiritual Blindness** – Holding onto offense can make us feel powerful, but it actually keeps us in chains.
3. **The Desire for Justice** – We want people to pay for what they did, but forgiveness releases **God** to be the judge.
4. **Fear of Being Hurt Again** – Forgiveness doesn't always mean reconciliation, but many fear that forgiving will make them vulnerable.
5. **The Lies of the Enemy** – Satan deceives people into thinking that unforgiveness gives them control, when in reality, it controls them.

📖 2 Corinthians 2:10-11 – "Anyone you forgive, I also forgive... lest Satan should take advantage of us."

The enemy uses unforgiveness as a tool to bring division and pain, but Jesus calls us to live differently.

Forgiveness is Medicine for the Soul

Did you know that forgiveness is scientifically proven to bring healing? Studies show that holding onto bitterness can lead to:

• Increased stress and anxiety
• High blood pressure

- Weakened immune system
- Depression and emotional distress

📖 Proverbs 17:22 – "A joyful heart is good medicine, but a crushed spirit dries up the bones."

When you forgive, your heart is set free, and your body follows. Forgiveness is not just a spiritual act—it is also a healing act.

Who Does Forgiveness Help?

1. **It Helps You** – Forgiveness frees you from bitterness and allows God's peace to rule your heart.
2. **It Helps the Offender** – It gives them a chance to repent and experience grace.
3. **It Helps Your Relationship with God** – Unforgiveness blocks blessings, but forgiveness restores intimacy with Him.
4. **It Helps the World Around You** – Forgiveness transforms families, friendships, and communities.

📖 Colossians 3:13 – "Bear with each other and forgive one another if any of you has a grievance against someone. Forgive as the Lord forgave you."

Forgiveness is not just about the past—it shapes the future.

The Role of Prayer in Forgiveness

If forgiving someone seems too difficult, start with prayer.

📖 Mark 11:25 – "Whenever you stand praying, forgive, if you have anything against anyone."

Jesus ties prayer and forgiveness together because prayer changes our hearts. Sometimes, we must pray for the strength to forgive, and as we do, God softens our hearts.

The Ultimate Reward of Forgiveness

📖 Revelation 5:8 – "The prayers of the saints are incense before God."

Your forgiveness is not forgotten. Every time you forgive, God takes notice. The Bible says that forgiveness is connected to our eternal reward.

Forgiveness prepares us for heaven. It removes barriers between us and God, allowing us to live fully in His love and purpose.

Are You Ready to Be Free?

If you are holding onto pain, bitterness, or resentment, this book will guide you to freedom. It will show you how to walk in forgiveness, experience God's healing, and release every burden that has weighed you down.

Forgiveness is not just an act—it is a lifestyle of freedom. Jesus gave us the example, and now, He invites us to follow Him into a life of grace, peace, and restoration.

📖 Matthew 18:21-22 – "Lord, how often shall my brother sin against me, and I forgive him? Up to seven times?" Jesus said, "Not seven times, but seventy times seven."

The time to forgive is now. Let this journey begin.

Chapter 1: Understanding Forgiveness in the Bible

What is Forgiveness? A Biblical Definition

Forgiveness is one of the most fundamental principles in the Bible. It is not simply forgetting or excusing an offense, nor is it about pretending something never happened. Forgiveness is a conscious decision to release a person from the debt of their wrongdoing, regardless of whether they deserve it.

📖 *Matthew 6:14-15* – "For if you forgive other people when they sin against you, your heavenly Father will also forgive you. But if you do not forgive others their sins, your Father will not forgive your sins."

From this passage, we see that forgiveness is not optional for a believer. It is tied directly to receiving God's forgiveness for our own sins. When we refuse to forgive, we are, in essence, blocking the flow of God's mercy into our lives. This is a sobering reality, as it means that harboring unforgiveness can place a barrier between us and the grace of God.

Forgiveness in Scripture is often depicted as cancellation of debt (Matthew 18:23-35). Just as Christ canceled our debt of sin by His sacrifice on the cross, we are called to extend the same mercy to those who wrong us.

The Biblical Definition of Forgiveness:

1. To release someone from a debt or offense (Luke 7:41-42).
2. To show mercy instead of seeking vengeance (Romans 12:19).
3. To love our enemies as God loved us while we were still sinners (Romans 5:8).
4. To not hold resentment but entrust justice to God (Psalm 103:12).

True forgiveness is not about whether someone deserves it—it is about choosing obedience to God.

God's Perspective on Forgiveness

Forgiveness is at the heart of God's character. From Genesis to Revelation, we see a merciful God who offers forgiveness to humanity, even when we do not deserve it.

📖 *Psalm 103:12* – "As far as the east is from the west, so far has he removed our transgressions from us."

This verse illustrates God's limitless forgiveness. Unlike humans who struggle to let go of past hurts, God completely removes our sins from His sight. He does not hold them over us; instead, He restores us when we repent.

📖 *Isaiah 43:25* – "I, even I, am he who blots out your transgressions, for my own sake, and remembers your sins no more."

God's forgiveness is not based on our merit but on His own character. He forgives for His own sake, meaning that His love compels Him to offer grace freely. This is the same posture we must take toward others.

God's forgiveness is:

1. **Unconditional:** He forgives even before we ask (Luke 23:34).
2. **Sacrificial:** It cost Jesus His life (Ephesians 1:7).
3. **Restorative:** It brings healing and renewal (2 Chronicles 7:14).

If God, who is holy, extends grace to sinners, how much more should we, as imperfect humans, forgive one another?

Forgiveness vs. Reconciliation: Understanding the Difference

One of the biggest misconceptions about forgiveness is that it always leads to **reconciliation**. However, the two are not the same.

📖 *Romans 12:18* – "If it is possible, as far as it depends on you, live at peace with everyone."

This passage acknowledges that reconciliation is **not always possible**. While we are called to forgive unconditionally, reconciliation requires mutual effort and trust.

Key Differences Between Forgiveness and Reconciliation:

Forgiveness	Reconciliation
A one-sided decision to release offense	A mutual restoration of a relationship
Required by God	Encouraged but not always possible
Does not require the offender's apology	Requires both parties to agree
Frees the forgiver from bitterness	Restores the relationship to harmony

3

Forgiveness	Reconciliation
Based on God's command	Based on trust and repentance

Examples:

- If someone **betrays your trust**, you must forgive them, but it does not mean you must place yourself in a vulnerable position again.
- If someone **abuses you**, forgiveness is required, but reconciliation may not be wise without evidence of true repentance.

Reconciliation is always ideal, but forgiveness is always required.

Biblical Example: The Parable of the Unmerciful Servant (Matthew 18:21-35)

📖 *Matthew 18:21-22* – "Then Peter came to Jesus and asked, 'Lord, how many times shall I forgive my brother or sister who sins against me? Up to seven times?' Jesus answered, 'I tell you, not seven times, but seventy-seven times.'"

This passage begins with Peter asking how many times he must forgive. Jesus' response shows that forgiveness is unlimited. It is not about counting offenses but adopting a lifestyle of mercy.

📖 *Matthew 18:23-35* – Jesus tells the parable of a servant who owed an enormous debt to his master. The master forgave the debt out of compassion. However, this same servant refused to forgive a fellow servant who owed him a much smaller amount. When the master heard of this, he was enraged and threw the servant into prison.

Key Lessons from This Parable:

1. **God's Forgiveness is Greater than Any Offense Against Us.**

o   The servant's debt was impossible to repay—just like our debt of sin.

o   God **forgave us freely**, and we must extend that same grace.

2. **Unforgiveness is Hypocrisy.**

o   The servant was forgiven but refused to forgive.

o   When we refuse to forgive, we **deny the grace** we have received.

3. **Unforgiveness Imprisons Us.**

o   The unforgiving servant was thrown into prison.

o   Holding onto bitterness **chains us spiritually and emotionally**.

📖 *Matthew 18:35* – "This is how my heavenly Father will treat each of you unless you forgive your brother or sister from your heart."

This verse is a **serious warning**. If we refuse to forgive, we risk **losing God's forgiveness**.

Jesus Teaches That Forgiveness is Not Optional for Believers

📖 *Mark 11:25* – "And whenever you stand praying, forgive, if you have anything against anyone, so that your Father also who is in heaven may forgive you your trespasses."

Jesus emphasizes that forgiveness is a requirement, not a suggestion.

📖 *Luke 6:37* – "Forgive, and you will be forgiven."

God's forgiveness is **conditional** upon our willingness to forgive. When we hold onto offense, we **block** the blessings, peace, and mercy that God desires to pour into our lives.

Final Thoughts: Why We Must Forgive

Forgiveness is one of the most difficult yet most liberating things a believer can do. It is not about excusing sin—it is about releasing ourselves from the prison of bitterness.

📖 *Colossians 3:13* – "Bear with each other and forgive one another if any of you has a grievance against someone. Forgive as the Lord forgave you."

Key Takeaways:

1. Forgiveness is a Command, Not a Feeling.
2. It is an Act of Faith, Not Emotion.
3. It Sets You Free from the Pain of the Past.
4. It Restores Your Relationship with God.

♦ **Are you holding onto unforgiveness?** If so, ask God for the strength to release it today. Your breakthrough is on the other side of obedience.

📖 *Matthew 18:21-22* – *"How many times must I forgive?"* Jesus says, *"Seventy times seven."*

Forgive, and walk in freedom.

Chapter 2:
The Command to Forgive –
Why It's Not Optional

Forgiveness: A Command, Not a Choice

📖 Ephesians 4:32 – "Be kind to one another, tenderhearted, forgiving one another, as God in Christ forgave you."

Forgiveness is not optional for a believer. It is a direct command from God, modeled by Jesus, and required for those who follow Christ. While the world teaches that forgiveness is conditional—that people must earn it—God's standard is different. He commands us to forgive regardless of whether the person deserves it.

Forgiveness is often difficult because it requires us to surrender our right to justice and entrust that justice to God. When we hold onto bitterness, we become prisoners of our own unforgiveness, yet Jesus calls us to release the offense and walk in freedom.

Many believers struggle with forgiveness because they see it as an act of weakness. However, forgiveness is an act of spiritual strength. It requires humility, surrender, and obedience to God's Word. Unforgiveness keeps us tied to our pain, but forgiveness sets us free.

Jesus' Radical Command to Forgive

One of the most radical aspects of Jesus' ministry was His teaching on forgiveness. Unlike the religious leaders of His time, who emphasized punishment and justice, Jesus spoke of mercy, love, and grace.

📖 Matthew 5:44 – "But I say to you, love your enemies and pray for those who persecute you."

This command goes against human nature. Loving and forgiving an enemy is one of the most difficult things a person can do. Yet Jesus does not present this as an option—He commands it.

📖 Matthew 6:14-15 – "For if you forgive other people when they sin against you, your heavenly Father will also forgive you. But if you do not forgive others their sins, your Father will not forgive your sins."

This is one of the most sobering statements in the Bible. Our forgiveness from God is directly tied to our willingness to forgive others. This means that unforgiveness is a sin that hinders our relationship with God.

Forgiveness is not about excusing sin—it is about releasing ourselves from the burden of bitterness.

How Often Should We Forgive?

📖 *Matthew 18:21-22* – "Then Peter came to Jesus and asked, 'Lord, how many times shall I forgive my brother or sister who sins against me? Up to seven times?' Jesus answered, 'I tell you, not seven times, but seventy times seven.'"

Peter, like many of us, wanted to place a limit on forgiveness. In Jewish tradition, forgiving someone three times was considered generous. Peter thought he was being extra righteous by suggesting seven times. But Jesus responded with a shocking statement: Seventy times seven!

Jesus was not giving a mathematical limit (490 times) but rather stating that forgiveness should be unlimited. We are never to stop forgiving, because God never stops forgiving us.

Why does Jesus command us to forgive so many times?

1. Because God has forgiven us beyond measure.
2. Because bitterness is a trap, and forgiveness keeps us free.
3. Because forgiveness reflects the heart of God.

Biblical Example: Jesus on the Cross – The Ultimate Act of Forgiveness

📖 Luke 23:34 – "Father, forgive them, for they do not know what they do."

The greatest example of forgiveness in history took place on the cross. Jesus, though innocent, was falsely accused, beaten, mocked, and nailed to a cross. Instead of cursing His enemies, He prayed for them.

At that moment, Jesus demonstrated the deepest level of forgiveness:

- He forgave those who physically harmed Him.
- He forgave those who betrayed Him.
- He forgave those who mocked Him.
- He forgave even though no one asked for forgiveness.

📖 Romans 5:8 – "But God demonstrates His own love for us in this: While we were still sinners, Christ died for us."

This means that Jesus forgave us before we even repented. His love was unconditional, and His forgiveness was freely given.

If Jesus could forgive the ones who crucified Him, how much more should we forgive those who have wronged us?

True Forgiveness is Modeled by Jesus and Must Be Extended Even to Enemies

One of the hardest aspects of forgiveness is forgiving those who do not deserve it. But Jesus did not just teach about forgiveness—He lived it.

📖 *Matthew 5:7* – "Blessed are the merciful, for they will be shown mercy."

Mercy is not giving people what they deserve—it is giving them grace, even when they don't deserve it.

📖 *Colossians 3:13* – "Bear with each other and forgive one another if any of you has a grievance against someone. Forgive as the Lord forgave you."

This verse commands us to forgive as Christ forgave us. How did Christ forgive us?

- **Freely** – We didn't earn it.
- **Completely** – He removed our sins as far as the east is from the west.
- **Permanently** – He does not hold our sins against us.

We are called to forgive in the same way.

The Consequences of Unforgiveness

Many people refuse to forgive because they think it will punish the other person. However, unforgiveness is like drinking poison and expecting the other person to die.

Unforgiveness has serious spiritual, emotional, and physical consequences:

1. **Spiritual Consequences:**

o   It **blocks our prayers** (Mark 11:25).

o   It **hinders our relationship with God** (Matthew 6:15).

o   It **gives Satan a foothold** (2 Corinthians 2:10-11).

2. **Emotional Consequences:**

o   It leads to **bitterness and resentment**.

o   It causes **anxiety and depression**.

o   It **destroys peace and joy**.

3. **Physical Consequences:**

o   Studies show that **unforgiveness increases stress, high blood pressure, and heart disease**.

o   It weakens the immune system.

o   It causes chronic **fatigue and insomnia**.

Forgiveness is not just for the offender—it is for the one who was hurt. It brings healing and freedom.

Practical Steps to Forgive

Forgiveness can be difficult, but God gives us the strength to do it.

📖 *Philippians 4:13* – "I can do all things through Christ who strengthens me."

Here are practical steps to forgive:

1. **Pray for Strength** – Ask God to help you forgive (Mark 11:25).
2. **Let Go of the Pain** – Release the offense to God (Romans 12:19).
3. **Bless the Person Who Hurt You** – Speak life instead of bitterness (Luke 6:28).
4. **Remember God's Mercy Toward You** – Meditate on how much God has forgiven you (Colossians 3:13).
5. **Choose Forgiveness Daily** – It is a continuous decision, not a one-time event.

📖 2 Corinthians 5:17 – "Therefore, if anyone is in Christ, the new creation has come: The old has gone, the new is here!"

Forgiveness is a gift you give yourself. It releases you from the prison of the past and allows you to step into the freedom of the future.

Final Thoughts: Will You Choose to Obey?

Jesus has made it clear—**forgiveness is not optional.** It is a direct **command from God**, a reflection of His love, and a requirement for those who follow Him.

📖 *Mark 11:25* – "And when you stand praying, if you hold anything against anyone, forgive them, so that your Father in heaven may forgive you your sins."

◆ **Are you holding onto unforgiveness today?**

◆ **Will you obey God's command and forgive?**

Forgiveness is not about the other person—it is about your heart before God. Choose obedience. Choose freedom. Choose to forgive.

Chapter 3:
Why People Struggle to Forgive

📖 2 Corinthians 2:10-11 – "Anyone you forgive, I also forgive… lest Satan should take advantage of us."

Forgiveness is one of the most powerful, liberating acts a believer can walk in, yet it is also one of the hardest. Many struggle to forgive because of the pain of betrayal, the desire for justice, or even the fear of being hurt again. The world often teaches that forgiveness should only be given when it is deserved, yet the Bible commands us to forgive unconditionally, just as Christ forgave us.

If forgiveness is so freeing, why do so many people resist it? Why do people hold on to bitterness even when it destroys them? Understanding the reasons behind the struggle to forgive helps us identify and break free from the strongholds that keep us bound.

Common Reasons Why People Refuse to Forgive

While each person's journey to forgiveness is unique, there are common reasons why people struggle to let go of offenses. These roadblocks to forgiveness must be recognized and surrendered to God in order for true healing to take place.

1. Deep Pain and Betrayal

One of the biggest reasons people struggle to forgive is because of how deeply they have been wounded. When someone experiences betrayal, rejection, abuse, or deception, the pain runs so deep that forgiveness feels impossible.

📖 *Psalm 55:12-14* – "If an enemy were insulting me, I could endure it; if a foe were rising against me, I could hide. But it is you, a man like myself, my companion, my close friend, with whom I once enjoyed sweet fellowship."

David's words describe the heartbreak of being wounded by someone close. Betrayal cuts the deepest when it comes from someone we loved and trusted.

Examples of Deep Betrayal in the Bible:

1. **Judas betrayed Jesus (Luke 22:47-48)** – Jesus was betrayed by one of His closest disciples.
2. **David was betrayed by his own son, Absalom (2 Samuel 15:10-14)** – Yet David still mourned for him.
3. **Peter denied Jesus three times (Luke 22:54-62)** – Instead of holding it against him, Jesus restored Peter (John 21).

Forgiving deep wounds does not mean excusing the sin, but rather releasing ourselves from the burden of carrying it. When we refuse to forgive because of pain, we remain chained to the very thing that hurt us.

📖 *Romans 12:19* – "Do not take revenge, my dear friends, but leave room for God's wrath."

Holding onto offense does not heal the wound—it keeps it open.

2. Pride and Spiritual Blindness

Pride is another major obstacle to forgiveness. Pride tells us that the person who hurt us does not deserve grace. It convinces us that if we forgive, we are letting them get away with it.

📖 *Proverbs 16:18* – "Pride goes before destruction, a haughty spirit before a fall."

Pride keeps people in bondage by whispering lies such as:

- "They don't deserve my forgiveness."
- "If I forgive them, they'll think they won."
- "I have a right to be angry."

However, the Bible warns us against harboring prideful unforgiveness.

📖 James 4:6 – "God opposes the proud but gives grace to the humble."

Pride convinces people that holding onto offense gives them power, but in reality, it keeps them enslaved.

Example of Spiritual Blindness:

In *Luke 15:25-32*, the older brother in the Prodigal Son parable refused to celebrate his younger brother's return because he was offended by the father's forgiveness. His pride blinded him to the beauty of grace.

Pride and unforgiveness go hand in hand. The more we resist forgiveness, the more spiritually blind we become.

3. The Desire for Revenge

Many struggle to forgive because they want the offender to suffer. When someone has deeply hurt us, the desire for justice and retribution can be overwhelming.

📖 *Matthew 5:38-39* – "You have heard that it was said, 'Eye for eye, and tooth for tooth.' But I tell you, do not resist an evil person. If anyone slaps you on the right cheek, turn to them the other cheek also."

Jesus rejected the law of revenge and replaced it with a law of mercy.

📖 *Romans 12:17-19* – "Do not repay anyone evil for evil… Do not take revenge, but leave room for God's wrath."

When we refuse to forgive, we take God's place as the judge.

Example of Revenge vs. Mercy:

- Joseph's brothers betrayed him, but he chose mercy (Genesis 50:15-21).
- David had the chance to kill Saul but spared his life (1 Samuel 24:10-12).

Forgiveness is about trusting God to handle justice.

The Three Stages of Unforgiveness

Unforgiveness does not always start as anger toward others. It often **begins with ourselves** and **spirals into deeper bitterness**.

1. Blaming Yourself

Many people struggle with forgiveness because they feel like **they should have known better**.

- "Why did I trust them?"
- "It's my fault I got hurt."

This self-condemnation keeps us trapped.

📖 *Romans 8:1* – "There is now no condemnation for those who are in Christ Jesus."

Forgiveness starts with accepting God's grace for ourselves.

2. Blaming Others

Once we stop blaming ourselves, we often shift to **blaming others**.

- "They ruined my life."
- "I'll never trust anyone again."

📖 *Ephesians 4:31* – "Get rid of all bitterness, rage, and anger."

Holding onto blame poisons our hearts.

3. Blaming God

The final stage of unforgiveness is **anger toward God**.

- "Why did God allow this?"
- "If God is good, why did this happen?"

📖 *Revelation 2:24* – Many **turn away from God** because of deep wounds.

But God is not the cause of our pain—He is the healer. Blaming God only prolongs our suffering.

Biblical Example: Joseph and His Brothers

📖 *Genesis 50:20* – "You intended to harm me, but God intended it for good."

Joseph had every reason to be bitter. His own brothers:

- Sold him into slavery.
- Lied about him to their father.
- Left him for dead.

Yet, when he finally had power over them, he chose mercy.

✓ Joseph forgave because he trusted God's greater plan.

When we forgive, we release the offender's control over our lives and walk in God's perfect peace.

Final Thoughts: Forgiveness is Freedom

Refusing to forgive only **hurts us**. It keeps us locked in the **past**, chained to **bitterness**, and blind to **God's healing power**.

📖 *John 8:36* – "So if the Son sets you free, you will be free indeed."

◆ Are you holding onto unforgiveness today?

◆ Will you let go and trust God to bring justice?

Forgiveness is not about forgetting. **It is about choosing freedom.**

Chapter 4:
The Spiritual Impact of Forgiveness

📖 Hebrews 12:15 – "See to it that no one falls short of the grace of God and that no bitter root grows up to cause trouble and defile many."

Forgiveness is not just a moral obligation or an emotional relief—it is a deeply spiritual act with eternal consequences. The Bible teaches that our ability to forgive directly impacts our relationship with God, our ability to receive His blessings, and our spiritual freedom. When we choose not to forgive, we open the door to spiritual attacks, emotional torment, and hindered prayers.

Many believers do not realize how unforgiveness can sever their connection with God. They see forgiveness as a personal issue, but in reality, it is a spiritual battle. The enemy knows that as long as we hold onto bitterness, we block God's power from flowing in our lives. Satan uses unforgiveness as a tool to keep us bound—preventing us from walking in the fullness of God's grace.

This chapter will explore the spiritual impact of unforgiveness, the devil's strategy to keep people in bondage, and how forgiveness restores alignment with God's will.

1. How Unforgiveness Severs Your Relationship with God

Many Christians believe that their personal grudges and unresolved offenses do not affect their spiritual lives, but the Bible teaches otherwise.

📖 Matthew 6:14-15 – *"For if you forgive other people when they sin against you, your heavenly Father will also forgive you. But if you do not forgive others their sins, your Father will not forgive your sins."*

This verse is not a suggestion—it is a clear spiritual law. If we refuse to forgive others, God will not forgive us. This means that unforgiveness disrupts our fellowship with God and blocks our access to His grace.

How Unforgiveness Creates Spiritual Distance from God

- **Unforgiveness blocks your prayers**

📖 Mark 11:25 – "And whenever you stand praying, forgive, if you have anything against anyone, so that your Father who is in heaven may forgive you your trespasses."

Unforgiveness makes our prayers ineffective. If we harbor bitterness, God withholds His response until we release the offense.

- **Unforgiveness hinders worship**

📖 Matthew 5:23-24 – "If you are offering your gift at the altar and there remember that your brother has something against you, leave your gift there before the altar and go. First be reconciled to your brother, and then come and offer your gift."

21

God does not accept our worship when our hearts are full of unforgiveness. Before we can truly connect with Him, we must first let go of bitterness.

Unforgiveness grieves the Holy Spirit

- 📖 Ephesians 4:30-32 – "Do not grieve the Holy Spirit of God… Get rid of all bitterness, rage, and anger… Be kind and compassionate to one another, forgiving each other, just as in Christ God forgave you."

The Holy Spirit is sensitive to our heart conditions. When we refuse to forgive, we quench His presence in our lives.

✓ Forgiveness restores our connection with God. When we release offenses, we invite God's peace, joy, and presence back into our hearts.

2. Satan's Strategy: Using Unforgiveness to Block Blessings

📖 2 Corinthians 2:11 – "Lest Satan should take advantage of us; for we are not ignorant of his devices."

Satan understands the spiritual laws of forgiveness better than many believers do. That is why he constantly tempts people to hold onto grudges, dwell in bitterness, and resist reconciliation.

How Satan Uses Unforgiveness to Keep People in Bondage

1. Unforgiveness Gives the Devil a Foothold

📖 Ephesians 4:26-27 – "In your anger do not sin: Do not let the sun go down while you are still angry, and do not give the devil a foothold."

Every time we harbor unforgiveness, we open a door for demonic oppression. The enemy thrives in environments of bitterness and resentment.

3.Unforgiveness Keeps People in Emotional and Spiritual Captivity

📖 Matthew 18:34-35 – "In anger, his master handed him over to the jailers to be tortured until he should pay back all he owed. This is how my heavenly Father will treat each of you unless you forgive your brother from your heart."

Jesus describes unforgiveness as spiritual imprisonment. Many people experience anxiety, depression, and torment because they refuse to forgive.

4.Unforgiveness Blocks Financial and Spiritual Blessings

📖 Luke 6:37-38 – "Forgive, and you will be forgiven. Give, and it will be given to you... For with the measure you use, it will be measured to you."

God blesses those who walk in forgiveness. If we hold onto bitterness, we block the overflow of God's provision in our lives.

✅ Forgiveness breaks Satan's power and unlocks blessings. The moment we release offenses, we destroy strongholds that have kept us bound.

5 The Difference Between Conviction and Condemnation

📖 Romans 8:1 – "There is now no condemnation for those in Christ Jesus."

Many people resist forgiveness because they confuse conviction with condemnation.

Conviction vs. Condemnation

Conviction (From the Holy Spirit)	Condemnation (From the Enemy)
Leads to repentance and healing	Leads to shame and hopelessness
Brings clarity and guidance	Brings confusion and despair
Restores relationship with God	Creates distance from God
Encourages change and growth	Encourages self-hatred

How the Enemy Uses Condemnation to Block Forgiveness

1. **He convinces people that their sin is too great to be forgiven.**

📖 1 John 1:9 – "If we confess our sins, He is faithful and just to forgive us our sins and to cleanse us from all unrighteousness."

2. **He keeps people trapped in guilt and regret.**

📖 Psalm 103:12 – "As far as the east is from the west, so far has He removed our transgressions from us."

3. **He discourages people from seeking God's mercy.**

📖 Lamentations 3:22-23 – "His mercies never come to an end; they are new every morning."

✓ God does not condemn—He redeems. The moment we choose forgiveness, we break the chains of condemnation and walk in God's love.

4. Forgiveness Restores Spiritual Alignment

Forgiveness is not just about **letting go of the past**—it is about **realigning our hearts with God's will**.

📖 **Colossians 3:13** – *"Bear with each other and forgive one another... Forgive as the Lord forgave you."*

How Forgiveness Restores Our Spiritual Lives

1. Forgiveness Allows the Holy Spirit to Move Freely

📖 Galatians 5:22-23 – "The fruit of the Spirit is love, joy, peace, forbearance, kindness, goodness, faithfulness, gentleness and self-control."

2. Forgiveness Restores Joy and Peace

📖 Isaiah 26:3 – "You will keep in perfect peace those whose minds are steadfast, because they trust in you."

3. Forgiveness Strengthens Our Faith

📖 Matthew 21:22 – "If you believe, you will receive whatever you ask for in prayer."

✓ Forgiveness is the key to spiritual breakthrough. When we forgive, we align ourselves with the heart of God and step into His divine purpose.

Final Thoughts: The Freedom of Forgiveness

📖 **John 8:36** – "So if the Son sets you free, you will be free indeed."

✅ **Are you willing to break free from unforgiveness today?**

✅ **Will you trust God to handle justice?**

Forgiveness is not about **forgetting the pain**—it is about **choosing freedom over bondage**. When you **let go of bitterness**, heaven **moves on your behalf**.

Chapter 5:
The Physical and Emotional
Effects of Unforgiveness

📖 Proverbs 17:22 – "A joyful heart is good medicine, but a crushed spirit dries up the bones."

Forgiveness is often thought of as a spiritual and moral choice, but few realize that it has direct effects on our physical and emotional well-being. Holding onto bitterness, resentment, and grudges does not just affect relationships—it damages the body and mind.

Medical research and biblical wisdom both confirm that unforgiveness is toxic. It leads to stress, high blood pressure, anxiety, depression, and even chronic illness. Conversely, choosing forgiveness promotes healing, lowers stress, and restores emotional peace.

The Bible teaches that forgiveness is not just a command—it is a gift to ourselves. In this chapter, we will explore:

1. The scientific connection between unforgiveness and physical health.
2. How bitterness and resentment increase stress, anxiety, and disease.
3. The healing power of forgiveness and why it is like medicine for the soul.
4. Biblical examples of physical restoration after forgiving others.

27

1. The Science of Forgiveness: How Bitterness Affects Your Body

📖 Proverbs 14:30 – "A tranquil heart gives life to the flesh, but envy makes the bones rot."

Forgiveness is not just about spiritual freedom—it affects our brain, immune system, and overall health.

How Unforgiveness Affects the Body

When we hold onto **unforgiveness**, our body releases **stress hormones** like cortisol and adrenaline. These chemicals are useful in emergencies, but when released **consistently due to stress or resentment**, they start breaking down the body.

1. **Increased Blood Pressure & Heart Disease**

o Chronic **anger and resentment** lead to **hypertension (high blood pressure)**.

o Studies show that people who hold grudges have **a greater risk of heart attacks and strokes**.

2. **Weakened Immune System**

o Long-term bitterness suppresses the immune system.

o The body **prioritizes stress response over healing**, making people prone to infections and slow recovery.

3. **Digestive Issues & Stomach Problems**

o Anger and stress lead to **inflammation in the gut**, causing ulcers, acid reflux, and irritable bowel syndrome.

4. **Increased Pain & Chronic Illness**

o   Studies link **unforgiveness to higher levels of chronic pain**.

o   Holding onto anger contributes to conditions like **fibromyalgia and migraines**.

📖 **Biblical Perspective:**

📖 Psalm 32:3-4 – "When I kept silent, my bones wasted away through my groaning all day long. For day and night Your hand was heavy upon me; my strength was sapped as in the heat of summer."

✅ The body reflects what is happening in the soul. When we harbor unforgiveness, our health suffers. But when we release bitterness, healing begins.

2. The Link Between Unforgiveness and Stress

📖 **Colossians 3:13** – "Bear with each other and forgive one another if any of you has a grievance against someone. Forgive as the Lord forgave you."

How Unforgiveness Creates Stress & Anxiety

Unforgiveness **keeps our minds in a state of constant stress**, creating anxiety, tension, and emotional instability.

The Three Stress Responses of Unforgiveness

1. **Fight Mode (Anger & Revenge)**

o   The person constantly **thinks about the offense**.

o   Leads to **hostility, irritability, and outbursts of anger**.

2. **Flight Mode (Emotional Numbness)**

o   The person **avoids relationships** to prevent more hurt.

29

o Leads to **isolation, depression, and disconnection from others**.

3. **Freeze Mode (Living in the Past)**

o The person replays the offense in their mind.

o Leads to **inability to move forward and make healthy decisions**.

📖 Biblical Warning: 📖 Hebrews 12:15 – "See to it that no one falls short of the grace of God and that no bitter root grows up to cause trouble and defile many."

✔ Bitterness spreads and affects every area of life. It causes stress, poisons relationships, and makes people miserable. But forgiveness stops the cycle.

3. Unforgiveness, Depression, and Mental Health

📖 Isaiah 26:3 – "You will keep in perfect peace those whose minds are steadfast, because they trust in You."

When we refuse to forgive, our mental health suffers. Research shows a strong link between unforgiveness and depression.

How Unforgiveness Causes Depression

- Keeps the brain in a negative loop (obsessing over the offense).
- Triggers feelings of helplessness and victimhood.
- Causes lack of motivation, joy, and purpose.
- Disconnects us from God's peace and emotional healing.

How Forgiveness Improves Mental Health

- Lowers depression and anxiety symptoms.

- Releases emotional burdens and promotes joy.
- Restores relationships and encourages peace.
- Increases self-worth and spiritual freedom.

📖 Biblical Example: Job Prayed for His Friends and Was Restored 📖 Job 42:10 – "After Job had prayed for his friends, the Lord restored his fortunes and gave him twice as much as he had before."

✓ When Job forgave and prayed for his friends, his restoration began. The same principle applies today—when we release offenses, God brings emotional and spiritual renewal.

4. Forgiveness as Medicine: The Healing Power of Releasing Offenses

📖 **Matthew 11:28** – "Come to Me, all who are weary and burdened, and I will give you rest."

Jesus invites us to **let go of burdens** and receive **healing through forgiveness**. Forgiveness is not just **letting go**—it is an **act of faith** that releases God's healing power.

How Forgiveness Heals the Body

1. **Lowers Blood Pressure & Reduces Stress**

o Studies show that **forgiving people have lower heart rates**.

o **Stress hormones decrease** when we stop replaying offenses.

2. **Boosts the Immune System**

o Forgiveness **reduces inflammation** and helps the body fight infections.

o   People who forgive **recover faster from sickness**.

3.   **Promotes Brain Health**

o   Studies show **forgiveness improves memory, focus, and cognitive function**.

o   Holding onto resentment **creates mental fog and exhaustion**.

📖 Scientific Support for Forgiveness as Medicine ♦ Dr. Everett Worthington, a clinical psychologist, found that forgiveness reduces stress, lowers anxiety, and improves heart health. ♦ The American Psychological Association confirms that forgiveness improves emotional well-being and extends lifespan.

📖 Biblical Principle: 📖 *Proverbs 3:7-8 – "Do not be wise in your own eyes; fear the Lord and shun evil. This will bring health to your body and nourishment to your bones."*

♡ Forgiveness brings life, renewal, and peace. Holding onto bitterness leads to spiritual, emotional, and physical decay.

5. Choosing Forgiveness Brings Mental and Physical Renewal

📖 Philippians 4:7 – "And the peace of God, which surpasses all understanding, will guard your hearts and your minds in Christ Jesus."

When we choose forgiveness, we experience God's peace, restoration, and healing.

How to Start the Forgiveness Process

1.   **Make a Decision to Forgive**

o   Forgiveness is a **choice, not a feeling**.

o   📖 *Colossians 3:13 – "Forgive as the Lord forgave you."*

2. **Pray for the Person Who Hurt You**

o   📖 *Matthew 5:44 – "Love your enemies and pray for those who persecute you."*

o   Praying for others **heals the heart and softens bitterness**.

3. **Replace Negative Thoughts with Scripture**

o   📖 *Romans 12:2 – "Be transformed by the renewing of your mind."*

o   Meditate on **God's promises of peace**.

✅ Forgiveness is the key to healing. When we let go, we invite God's supernatural peace into our hearts.

Final Thoughts: The Power of Letting Go

📖 **John 8:36** – "So if the Son sets you free, you will be free indeed."

✅ **Forgiveness is for YOU. It brings healing, peace, and joy.**

✅ **Are you ready to let go and receive God's restoration?**

📖 "A joyful heart is good medicine." (Proverbs 17:22)

◆ **Forgive today—your body, mind, and soul will thank you.** ◆

Chapter 6:
The Power of Forgiving Yourself

📖 1 John 1:9 – "If we confess our sins, He is faithful and just to forgive us our sins and to cleanse us from all unrighteousness."

One of the greatest barriers to healing and freedom is the inability to forgive oneself. Many people believe in God's forgiveness, yet they struggle with guilt, shame, and self-condemnation. This is because the enemy attacks the mind, convincing people that their mistakes define them, that they are unworthy of restoration, or that they have failed beyond redemption.

However, the Bible clearly teaches that God's forgiveness is greater than our failures. No sin is too great that God's grace cannot cover it. If God, who is holy and just, is willing to forgive us, then why do we struggle to forgive ourselves?

In this chapter, we will explore:

- Why people struggle to forgive themselves.
- The difference between God's mercy and self-condemnation.
- Biblical examples of self-forgiveness vs. self-destruction.
- How to break free from guilt and embrace God's restoration.

1. Why Do People Struggle to Forgive Themselves?

📖 Romans 8:1 – "There is now no condemnation for those who are in Christ Jesus."

Self-forgiveness is difficult because the mind and heart often hold onto guilt long after God has forgiven us. People struggle with self-condemnation for several reasons:

1. They Feel That Their Sin is Too Big to Forgive

- Many people believe they have **gone too far** for God's grace.
- The enemy whispers **lies of condemnation**, making them feel **permanently stained**.

📖 Biblical Example: Paul the Apostle 📖 1 Timothy 1:15 – *"Christ Jesus came into the world to save sinners—of whom I am the worst."* ✅ Paul had persecuted Christians, yet God forgave him and used him to write much of the New Testament.

2. They Think They Must "Earn" Forgiveness

- Some people feel they must suffer enough before they can be forgiven.
- This belief is rooted in works, not grace.

📖 **Ephesians 2:8-9** – "For it is by grace you have been saved, through faith—and this is not from yourselves, it is the gift of God—not by works, so that no one can boast." ✅ **God's grace is a gift**, not something we can **earn**.

3. They Replay Their Mistakes Over and Over

- The mind replays failures, keeping people trapped in the past.
- This is a tactic of Satan, who is called the accuser of the brethren (Revelation 12:10).

📖 **Isaiah 43:18-19** – *"Forget the former things; do not dwell on the past. See, I am doing a new thing!"* ✅ **God does not dwell on our past mistakes**, so neither should we.

2. God's Mercy vs. Self-Condemnation

📖 Micah 7:18-19 – "Who is a God like You, who pardons sin and forgives the transgression of the remnant of His inheritance? You do not stay angry forever but delight to show mercy."

Many people believe God is holding their past sins against them, but the Bible clearly states that God delights in showing mercy. Self-condemnation is NOT from God—it is a tool of the enemy.

1. Understanding the Difference Between Conviction and Condemnation

- Conviction (from the Holy Spirit) leads to repentance and restoration.
- Condemnation (from Satan) leads to guilt and despair.

📖 Romans 8:34 – "Who then is the one who condemns? No one. Christ Jesus who died—more than that, who was raised to life—is at the right hand of God and is also interceding for us." ✅ If Jesus is interceding for us, why should we condemn ourselves?

2. God's Forgiveness is Absolute

- The Bible says when God forgives, He remembers our sins no more.
- 📖 Psalm 103:12 – "As far as the east is from the west, so far has He removed our transgressions from us."

✅ **If God has removed our sins, why do we hold onto them?**

3. Biblical Example: Peter's Denial vs. Judas' Betrayal

📖 Matthew 26:69-75 – Peter denied Jesus three times but was restored.

📖 Matthew 27:3-5 – Judas betrayed Jesus and took his own life.

Both Peter and Judas sinned against Jesus, yet their responses were very different. One found forgiveness and restoration, while the other fell into despair and self-condemnation.

1. Peter's Restoration

- Peter denied Jesus out of fear, but he repented and was restored.
- Jesus forgave him and commissioned him to lead the early church.

📖 John 21:15-17 – Jesus asked Peter three times, "Do you love Me?" and restored him.

✅ Peter learned that God's grace is greater than any failure.

2. Judas' Despair

- Judas betrayed Jesus and felt deep remorse.
- But instead of seeking forgiveness, he gave in to despair.

📖 Matthew 27:5 – *"Judas went away and hanged himself."* ✅ Judas let guilt destroy him instead of receiving God's mercy.

4. How to Break Free from Guilt and Self-Condemnation

📖 Psalm 34:18 – "The Lord is close to the brokenhearted and saves those who are crushed in spirit."

Many believers live under the weight of past mistakes, unable to move forward. But forgiveness includes forgiving yourself.

1. Accept God's Forgiveness

📖 Isaiah 1:18 – *"Though your sins are like scarlet, they shall be as white as snow."* ✅ No sin is greater than God's mercy. Accept His forgiveness fully.

2. Stop Replaying Past Mistakes

📖 Philippians 3:13 – *"Forgetting what is behind and straining toward what is ahead."* ✅ The past is over. Choose to move forward in faith.

3. Speak God's Truth Over Yourself

- Declare: "I am forgiven!" (1 John 1:9)
- Declare: "I am a new creation!" (2 Corinthians 5:17)

✅ Words have power. Speak life, not guilt.

4. Trust That God Has a Purpose for You

📖 Jeremiah 29:11 – *"For I know the plans I have for you, declares the Lord."* ✅ Your mistakes do not cancel God's plan for your life.

5. Replace Guilt with Worship

📖 Isaiah 61:3 – "He gives beauty for ashes, the oil of joy for mourning, and a garment of praise for a spirit of heaviness." ✅ When guilt weighs you down, worship lifts you up.

Final Thoughts: God's Forgiveness is Greater Than Your Failures

📖 **John 8:36** – "So if the Son sets you free, you will be free indeed."

✅ **If God has forgiven you, you must forgive yourself.**

✅ **Let go of the past and step into God's grace.**

📖 "There is now no condemnation for those who are in Christ Jesus." (Romans 8:1)

◆ **Forgive yourself today—God already has.** ◆

Chapter 7:
The Role of Prayer in Forgiveness

📖 Mark 11:25 – "And whenever you stand praying, forgive, if you have anything against anyone, so that your Father who is in heaven may forgive you your trespasses."

Forgiveness is not a one-time event; it is a daily discipline that must be practiced through prayer. Many people struggle to forgive because they try to do it in their own strength rather than through God's power. However, the Bible is clear that forgiveness is closely tied to prayer. Prayer softens the heart, aligns us with God's mercy, and releases the supernatural power needed to forgive.

In this chapter, we will explore:

- Why forgiveness must be a daily prayer.
- How prayer strengthens the heart to forgive.
- The biblical example of Stephen, who prayed for his enemies while being martyred.
- How prayer aligns our heart with God's mercy.

Forgiveness is not always easy, but prayer gives us the strength to do what is impossible in the flesh.

1. Why Must Forgiveness Be a Daily Prayer?

📖 Matthew 6:12 – "Forgive us our debts, as we also have forgiven our debtors."

Jesus included forgiveness in the Lord's Prayer, showing that it is something we must regularly ask for and extend to others.

1. Unforgiveness Can Become a Spiritual Blockage

- Unforgiveness hinders our relationship with God.
- It blocks our prayers from being answered.

📖 **Matthew 6:14-15** – "For if you forgive others their trespasses, your heavenly Father will also forgive you, but if you do not forgive others their trespasses, neither will your Father forgive your trespasses."

✓ Forgiveness is not optional; it is a requirement for a strong prayer life.

2. People Hurt Us Continually – We Must Forgive Continually

- Forgiveness is not a one-time decision but a daily surrender.
- Jesus taught that we must forgive repeatedly.

📖 **Matthew 18:21-22** – "Peter came up and said to Him, 'Lord, how often will my brother sin against me, and I forgive him? As many as seven times?' Jesus said to him, 'I do not say to you seven times, but seventy-seven times.'"

✓ Forgiveness is a daily decision, made possible through prayer.

3. Prayer Releases Bitterness Before It Takes Root

- Unforgiveness turns into bitterness, which is dangerous to the soul.
- Prayer prevents bitterness from taking root.

☐ **Hebrews 12:15** – "See to it that no one falls short of the grace of God and that no bitter root grows up to cause trouble and defile many."

✅ Through daily prayer, we uproot bitterness before it destroys us.

2. How Prayer Strengthens the Heart to Forgive

☐ **Luke 6:27-28** – "Love your enemies, do good to those who hate you, bless those who curse you, pray for those who mistreat you."

Forgiveness is not easy, especially when the wound is fresh. However, prayer gives us supernatural strength to forgive.

1. Prayer Connects You to God's Mercy

- When we spend time in God's presence, we are reminded of how much He has forgiven us.
- Prayer shifts our focus from the offense to God's grace.

☐ **Lamentations 3:22-23** – "The steadfast love of the Lord never ceases; His mercies never come to an end; they are new every morning."

✅ The more we focus on God's mercy, the more we are able to extend mercy to others.

2. Prayer Softens the Heart

- A hardened heart refuses to forgive, but prayer makes the heart tender.
- Spending time with God melts pride and anger.

📖 Ezekiel 36:26 – "And I will give you a new heart, and a new spirit I will put within you. And I will remove the heart of stone from your flesh and give you a heart of flesh."

✓ Prayer allows God to transform a hardened heart into one full of love and forgiveness.

3. Prayer Helps You See the Offender Through God's Eyes

• When we pray, God gives us His perspective.
• We begin to see that the person who hurt us is also in need of grace.

📖 **Luke 23:34** – "Father, forgive them, for they do not know what they are doing."

✓ Jesus prayed for His enemies because He saw beyond their actions—He saw their spiritual blindness.

3. Biblical Example: Stephen's Prayer While Being Stoned

📖 Acts 7:59-60 – "And as they were stoning Stephen, he called out, 'Lord Jesus, receive my spirit.' And falling to his knees, he cried out with a loud voice, 'Lord, do not hold this sin against them.'"

One of the most powerful examples of prayer and forgiveness in the Bible is Stephen, the first Christian martyr.

1. Stephen Was Being Killed, Yet He Prayed for His Killers

• Stephen was falsely accused, dragged out of the city, and stoned to death.
• Instead of cursing his executioners, he prayed for them.

✅ Only a heart filled with prayer could forgive in such a moment.

2. His Prayer Reflected the Heart of Jesus

- Stephen's final words echoed Jesus' prayer on the cross.
- He did not hold onto hatred, even in his last moments.

✅ Prayer had shaped his heart so deeply that even death could not steal his love.

3. Stephen's Forgiveness Opened the Door for God's Grace

- One of the men present at Stephen's stoning was Saul, who later became the Apostle Paul.
- Stephen's prayer may have planted a seed in Paul's heart, leading to his eventual conversion.

✅ Forgiveness through prayer not only frees the victim but also has the power to transform the offender.

4. How Prayer Aligns Your Heart with God's Mercy

📖 Matthew 5:7 – "Blessed are the merciful, for they shall receive mercy."

Prayer aligns our hearts with God's heart. When we spend time in prayer, we are filled with His love, making forgiveness possible.

1. Prayer Removes the Desire for Revenge

- Without prayer, it is easy to desire payback.
- Prayer changes the heart, replacing vengeance with peace.

📖 Romans 12:19 – "Do not take revenge, my dear friends, but leave room for God's wrath."

✔ Prayer shifts our battles to God, who fights for us.

2. Prayer Keeps You in a Place of Grace

- The more we pray, the more we walk in grace.
- Grace flows from God to us and then from us to others.

📖 Colossians 3:13 – "Bear with each other and forgive one another if any of you has a grievance against someone. Forgive as the Lord forgave you."

✔ Forgiveness is a gift we receive from God and must extend to others.

3. Prayer Helps You Move Forward

- Unforgiveness keeps you stuck in the past.
- Prayer empowers you to move forward into healing.

📖 Philippians 3:13-14 – "Forgetting what lies behind and straining forward to what lies ahead, I press on toward the goal."

✔ Through prayer, we release the past and step into God's future.

Final Thoughts: The Power of Prayer in Forgiveness

📖 Psalm 66:18 – "If I had cherished iniquity in my heart, the Lord would not have listened."

Prayer and forgiveness are deeply connected. Unforgiveness blocks our prayers, while forgiveness releases heaven's power.

◆ Through prayer, we receive the strength to forgive.

◆ Through forgiveness, we walk in freedom.

◆ Through freedom, we experience God's full blessings.

📖 "And whenever you stand praying, forgive." (Mark 11:25)

✓ Let go, pray, and walk in God's mercy today!

Chapter 8:
The Connection Between
Forgiveness and Healing

📖 James 5:16 – "Confess your sins to one another and pray for one another, that you may be healed. The prayer of a righteous person has great power as it is working."

Forgiveness and healing are deeply interconnected in both the spiritual and physical realms. Many people do not realize that unforgiveness can be a major hindrance to healing—whether it is emotional, physical, or spiritual healing. The Bible teaches that when we forgive, we create space for God's supernatural power to flow into our lives.

In this chapter, we will explore:

- How healing is connected to forgiveness.
- How unforgiveness creates spiritual blockages that prevent miracles.
- The biblical example of Jesus healing the paralyzed man by first forgiving his sins.
- The supernatural power released when we forgive others.

Forgiveness is not just an act of obedience—it is a pathway to complete healing and restoration.

1. Healing Is Connected to Forgiveness

📖 Matthew 9:2 – "And behold, some people brought to Him a paralytic, lying on a bed. And when Jesus saw their faith, He said to the paralytic, 'Take heart, my son; your sins are forgiven.'"

1. The Link Between Forgiveness and Physical Healing

The Bible reveals that sin and unforgiveness can be barriers to healing. Jesus often tied healing to the forgiveness of sins. Many times, before performing a miracle, He first declared forgiveness over the person.

- When we harbor unforgiveness, it creates spiritual and emotional burdens.
- Bitterness and resentment affect our body and mind, causing stress, anxiety, and even physical illness.
- When we release forgiveness, it opens the door for God's healing power to flow.

📖 Psalm 103:2-3 – "Bless the Lord, O my soul, and forget not all His benefits—who forgives all your iniquities, who heals all your diseases."

✓ Forgiveness is often the missing key to experiencing true healing.

2. The Science of Forgiveness and Healing

Even **scientific studies confirm** that unforgiveness has negative effects on our **physical health**.

- Unforgiveness can increase stress levels, leading to high blood pressure, heart disease, and immune system issues.

- Bitterness releases toxic chemicals in the body, increasing inflammation and the risk of diseases.
- Studies show that people who practice forgiveness experience lower stress, better heart health, and improved mental well-being.

🕮 **Proverbs 17:22** – "A joyful heart is good medicine, but a crushed spirit dries up the bones."

✅ When we forgive, we allow our hearts to be filled with peace and healing.

2. Unforgiveness as a Spiritual Block to Miracles

🕮 Mark 11:25 – "And whenever you stand praying, forgive, if you have anything against anyone, so that your Father who is in heaven may forgive you your trespasses."

1. Unforgiveness Hinders Prayers

Many people wonder why they are not receiving answers to their prayers. One reason may be that unforgiveness is blocking their access to God's power.

🕮 Isaiah 59:2 – *"But your iniquities have separated you from your God; your sins have hidden His face from you so that He will not hear."*

- Unforgiveness is a sin that creates a barrier between us and God.
- Until we forgive, our prayers can be hindered.
- When we release forgiveness, heaven opens, and God's power flows freely.

✓ If you feel like your prayers are not being answered, ask yourself: Is there someone I need to forgive?

2. Unforgiveness Blocks the Flow of God's Healing Power

📖 Matthew 6:14-15 – "For if you forgive others their trespasses, your heavenly Father will also forgive you, but if you do not forgive others their trespasses, neither will your Father forgive your trespasses."

- God desires to heal us, but bitterness and resentment block His blessings.
- The more we hold onto past hurts, the more we limit God's ability to heal us.
- Forgiveness removes the spiritual blockage and allows God's healing touch to flow.

📖 Ephesians 4:31-32 – "Let all bitterness and wrath and anger and clamor and slander be put away from you, along with all malice. Be kind to one another, tenderhearted, forgiving one another, as God in Christ forgave you."

✓ Forgiving others is a key to unlocking God's healing power in our lives.

3. Biblical Example: Jesus Heals the Paralyzed Man by First Forgiving Him

📖 Mark 2:5-11 – "When Jesus saw their faith, He said to the paralytic, 'Son, your sins are forgiven.' But some of the scribes were sitting there, questioning in their hearts… 'Who can forgive sins but God alone?'"

One of the most powerful examples of forgiveness and healing is found in Mark 2.

1. Jesus Prioritized Forgiveness Before Healing

- A paralyzed man was brought to Jesus for healing.
- Instead of immediately healing his body, Jesus first forgave his sins.
- The religious leaders were shocked, but Jesus showed that forgiveness is the foundation of true healing.

✔ Before the man could walk physically, he needed spiritual healing through forgiveness.

2. The Power of Faith in Forgiveness and Healing

- The man's friends had faith that Jesus could heal.
- Their faith moved Jesus to respond.

📖 Luke 5:20 – "When He saw their faith, He said, 'Friend, your sins are forgiven.'"

✔ Faith and forgiveness work together to bring total healing.

4. Forgiving Others Opens the Door to Supernatural Healing

📖 Luke 6:37 – "Forgive, and you will be forgiven."

1. Testimonies of Healing Through Forgiveness

Many believers have experienced miraculous healing when they finally let go of unforgiveness.

- A woman suffering from chronic illness found healing when she forgave her abusive father.

- A man with severe anxiety and depression was set free after releasing years of resentment against his ex-wife.
- A cancer patient experienced remission after asking God to help him forgive those who hurt him.

📖 Matthew 5:7 – "Blessed are the merciful, for they shall receive mercy."

✅ When we extend mercy, we receive healing mercy from God.

2. Forgiveness and Deliverance from Emotional Pain

- Many people suffer from deep emotional wounds.
- Forgiveness brings emotional and spiritual freedom.
- Letting go of past offenses allows God's peace to flood our hearts.

📖 Philippians 4:7 – "And the peace of God, which surpasses all understanding, will guard your hearts and your minds in Christ Jesus."

✅ Forgiveness releases us from emotional prisons and brings true peace.

Final Thoughts: Forgiveness Unlocks Healing

📖 Jeremiah 17:14 – "Heal me, O Lord, and I shall be healed; save me, and I shall be saved, for You are my praise."

Forgiveness and healing go hand in hand. When we release others, we make room for God's healing power.

✅ Forgiveness is the missing key to receiving divine healing.

✅ Unforgiveness blocks miracles—releasing it unlocks God's power.

✅ When we forgive, we step into complete emotional, physical, and spiritual healing.

📖 *"Confess your sins to one another and pray for one another, that you may be healed."* (James 5:16)

✅ Forgive, pray, and step into your healing today!

Chapter 9:
Overcoming Bitterness Through Forgiveness

📖 Colossians 3:13 – "Bear with each other and forgive one another if any of you has a grievance against someone. Forgive as the Lord forgave you."

Bitterness is one of the most dangerous poisons to the soul. It is a spiritual and emotional cancer that, if left unchecked, can consume a person's joy, relationships, and spiritual growth. Bitterness is unforgiveness turned inward, a deep-seated resentment that grows like a weed in the heart, strangling peace and love.

Many people carry bitterness unknowingly. It manifests through anger, resentment, distrust, and emotional walls built to protect from further hurt. Yet, in the process of guarding the heart, bitterness imprisons the soul. The only way to break free is through forgiveness, which is not just a command from God—it is a gift of healing for the one who forgives.

In this chapter, we will explore:

- The signs of bitterness and how it impacts the heart.
- How obedience to Christ leads to freedom from bitterness.
- A biblical example: Naomi's bitterness and Ruth's redemption.
- How forgiveness removes the stronghold of bitterness and restores joy.

Forgiveness is not ignoring the pain—it is choosing to release it so that God can bring healing and restoration.

1. Signs of Bitterness: How to Recognize It in Your Life

📖 Hebrews 12:15 – "See to it that no one falls short of the grace of God and that no bitter root grows up to cause trouble and defile many."

Bitterness does not appear overnight—it develops over time as a result of unforgiveness, unresolved pain, and disappointment. Like a root system underground, it spreads in the heart, eventually surfacing in behaviors and attitudes.

1. Anger and Resentment

Bitterness is often masked as justified anger. It comes when a person feels deeply wronged but refuses to let go of the offense.

- Do you replay past hurts over and over in your mind?
- Do you feel resentful when you see or hear about someone who hurt you?
- Are you easily angered when certain topics related to past pain come up?

📖 Ephesians 4:31 – "Get rid of all bitterness, rage and anger, brawling and slander, along with every form of malice."

✓ Unforgiveness keeps wounds fresh, while forgiveness allows them to heal.

2. Distrust and Emotional Walls

Bitterness builds walls instead of bridges. It leads to a hardened heart, making it difficult to trust others or even trust God.

- Do you struggle to form deep relationships because of past betrayals?
- Do you find yourself keeping people at a distance, afraid of being hurt again?
- Has your trust in God been affected because of past disappointments?

📖 Proverbs 4:23 – "Above all else, guard your heart, for everything you do flows from it."

✓ Bitterness does not protect the heart—it imprisons it. Forgiveness is the key to freedom.

2. Overcoming Bitterness Through Obedience to Christ

📖 Matthew 6:14-15 – "For if you forgive others their trespasses, your heavenly Father will also forgive you. But if you do not forgive others their trespasses, neither will your Father forgive your trespasses."

1. The Power of Obedience in Forgiveness

Forgiveness is not a feeling—it is a decision. Many people struggle with bitterness because they are waiting to feel ready to forgive. But forgiveness is an act of obedience, not an emotion.

- Jesus did not wait until He felt good to forgive those who crucified Him—He forgave while still in pain (Luke 23:34).
- Forgiveness is an act of faith, trusting that God will deal with justice while you receive peace.
- When you forgive, you release yourself from bondage and allow God to work in the situation.

📖 Romans 12:19 – "Do not take revenge, my dear friends, but leave room for God's wrath."

✓ Forgiveness is not letting someone off the hook—it is placing them in God's hands.

2. Releasing Bitterness Through Prayer

Prayer is one of the most powerful tools in overcoming bitterness. Jesus taught that we should pray even for those who hurt us.

📖 Matthew 5:44 – *"But I tell you, love your enemies and pray for those who persecute you."*

- When you pray for someone, it softens your heart toward them.
- Prayer allows God to change your heart and, if possible, restore broken relationships.
- Prayer brings divine healing, breaking bitterness and replacing it with peace and joy.

✓ Bitterness thrives in silence but dies in prayer. Start praying for those who hurt you.

3. Biblical Example: Naomi's Bitterness and Ruth's Redemption

📖 Ruth 1:20-21 – "Do not call me Naomi; call me Mara, for the Almighty has dealt very bitterly with me. I went away full, and the Lord has brought me back empty."

Naomi's story in the book of Ruth is a powerful example of how bitterness can take root—but also how God can redeem the brokenhearted.

1. Naomi's Loss and Bitterness

- Naomi lost her husband and both sons, leaving her a widow with no future.
- She became bitter toward God, believing He had abandoned her.
- She changed her name from Naomi ("pleasant") to Mara ("bitter").

📖 Psalm 34:18 – "The Lord is close to the brokenhearted and saves those who are crushed in spirit."

✓ Bitterness distorts our view of God, but He never stops working in our pain.

2. Ruth's Faithfulness and Naomi's Redemption

- Naomi's daughter-in-law, Ruth, chose to stay with her, showing unwavering love and forgiveness.
- Through Ruth, God restored Naomi's joy, leading her to redemption.
- Naomi went from bitterness to joy as she saw God's plan unfold.

📖 Ruth 4:14 – "Praise be to the Lord, who this day has not left you without a redeemer."

✓ Bitterness fades when we trust that God's plan is greater than our pain.

4. Forgiveness Removes the Stronghold of Bitterness

📖 Luke 6:37 – "Forgive, and you will be forgiven."

1. The Stronghold of Bitterness

A stronghold is a mindset or belief system that keeps us trapped. Bitterness becomes a spiritual stronghold when we:

- Dwell on past hurts instead of releasing them.
- Allow resentment to control our thoughts and actions.
- Refuse to surrender the pain to God.

📖 **2 Corinthians 10:4-5** – "The weapons of our warfare are not carnal but mighty in God for pulling down strongholds."

✅ Forgiveness breaks strongholds, releasing freedom and healing.

2. Choosing Freedom Over Bitterness

- Bitterness keeps you stuck—forgiveness sets you free.
- Bitterness blocks God's blessings—forgiveness opens heaven's doors.
- Bitterness destroys relationships—forgiveness restores them.

📖 John 8:36 – "So if the Son sets you free, you will be free indeed."

✅ Forgiveness is the key to walking in the freedom Jesus paid for.

Final Thoughts: Let Go and Live Free

📖 Ephesians 4:32 – "Be kind to one another, tenderhearted, forgiving one another, as God in Christ forgave you."

Bitterness is a silent thief—it steals joy, peace, and spiritual growth. But forgiveness is a gift that sets you free. Choose today to let go, trust God, and walk in the freedom of His love.

✓ Let go of past pain, and step into God's healing.

✓ Forgive, and live free.

Chapter 10:
The Role of Jesus in Forgiveness

📖 John 1:29 – "Behold, the Lamb of God, who takes away the sin of the world!"

Forgiveness is at the heart of Christianity, and Jesus Christ is the ultimate forgiver. His sacrifice on the cross was not just an act of love, but an act of divine justice, where He bore the punishment of all sin so that humanity could be reconciled to God.

Forgiveness is not merely about releasing offenses; it is about restoring broken relationships—first between God and mankind, and then between people. Without Jesus, there would be no true forgiveness because human efforts alone cannot erase the consequences of sin.

In this chapter, we will explore:

- Jesus as the ultimate forgiver.
- How His blood removes all sin and condemnation.
- A biblical example: The thief on the cross and Christ's mercy.
- How Jesus' forgiveness is the foundation of salvation.

Through Jesus, forgiveness is not just a possibility—it is a promise.

1. Jesus as the Ultimate Forgiver

📖 Luke 23:34 – "Father, forgive them, for they know not what they do."

Jesus did not just preach about forgiveness—He embodied it. His mission was clear: to reconcile humanity to God by taking away the sin of the world.

1. The Purpose of Jesus' Forgiveness

- Humanity was separated from God due to sin.
- The Law of Moses provided temporary sacrifices for sin, but Jesus became the final and perfect sacrifice (Hebrews 10:10).
- Through His blood, Jesus made forgiveness permanent and accessible to all who believe.

📖 Colossians 1:13-14 – "For He has rescued us from the dominion of darkness and brought us into the kingdom of the Son He loves, in whom we have redemption, the forgiveness of sins."

✓ Forgiveness through Jesus is not earned—it is received by faith.

2. Jesus Forgave Those Who Crucified Him

While suffering on the cross, Jesus had every reason to be angry and vengeful. Instead, He prayed for His executioners, saying, *"Father, forgive them."*

- His forgiveness was undeserved, yet freely given.
- Jesus forgave without waiting for an apology.
- He showed that forgiveness is an act of grace, not a response to repentance.

📖 1 Peter 2:23 – *"When they hurled their insults at Him, He did not retaliate; when He suffered, He made no threats. Instead, He entrusted Himself to Him who judges justly."*

✓ Jesus' example teaches us that forgiveness is an act of trust in God, not in the offender.

2. His Blood Removes All Sin and Condemnation

📖 Romans 8:1 – "There is therefore now no condemnation for those who are in Christ Jesus."

Many people struggle to forgive themselves because of shame and guilt. But the truth is that Jesus' sacrifice is more powerful than any sin.

1. The Blood of Jesus Cleanses from All Sin

Under the Old Testament, forgiveness was only granted through animal sacrifices (*Leviticus 17:11*). But Jesus became the final Lamb of God, removing sin completely.

📖 **Hebrews 9:22** – "Without the shedding of blood, there is no forgiveness of sins."

- The blood of animals could only cover sin temporarily.
- The blood of Jesus washes away sin permanently (1 John 1:7).

✓ There is no sin too great that the blood of Jesus cannot cleanse.

2. Jesus Removes Condemnation and Shame

Many people believe God is angry with them when they sin, but Jesus came to remove condemnation.

📖 John 3:17 – *"For God did not send His Son into the world to condemn the world, but to save the world through Him."*

- Condemnation comes from Satan (Revelation 12:10).
- Conviction comes from the Holy Spirit (John 16:8).
- Jesus removes guilt and restores righteousness (2 Corinthians 5:21).

✅ Forgiveness in Christ means you do not have to live in shame—you are made new.

3. Biblical Example: The Thief on the Cross

📖 Luke 23:39-43 – "Truly I tell you, today you will be with me in paradise."

One of the most powerful examples of Jesus' forgiveness was the thief on the cross.

1. The Two Responses to Jesus

- One thief mocked Jesus, saying, "If you are the Christ, save yourself and us."
- The other thief defended Jesus, saying, "We deserve this punishment, but this man has done nothing wrong."

✅ **True faith recognizes Jesus as Lord and acknowledges the need for forgiveness.**

2. Jesus' Immediate Forgiveness

The thief simply **asked for mercy**, saying, *"Lord, remember me when You come into Your kingdom."*

- Jesus did not require a religious ritual.

- Jesus did not demand good works.
- Jesus forgave him instantly and promised him eternal life.

📖 **Ephesians 2:8-9** – "For it is by grace you have been saved, through faith—and this is not from yourselves, it is the gift of God—not by works, so that no one can boast."

✅ **Salvation and forgiveness are gifts that can only be received by faith.**

4. Jesus' Forgiveness is the Foundation of Salvation

📖 Acts 4:12 – "Salvation is found in no one else, for there is no other name under heaven given to mankind by which we must be saved."

1. Why Salvation is Only Through Jesus

Many people try to find forgiveness through human efforts, but the Bible is clear that only Jesus can provide salvation.

- Religious rituals cannot save (Galatians 2:16).
- Good deeds cannot erase sin (Isaiah 64:6).
- Only Jesus' blood can remove sin completely (Hebrews 10:14).

📖 **John 14:6** – "I am the way, the truth, and the life. No one comes to the Father except through Me."

✅ Forgiveness is not about human effort—it is about trusting in Christ's finished work.

2. How to Receive Jesus' Forgiveness

To receive forgiveness, a person must:

1. **Acknowledge their sin (*Romans 3:23*).**

2. **Believe in Jesus' sacrifice (*Romans 10:9*).**

3. **Confess Jesus as Lord (*1 John 1:9*).**

📖 2 Corinthians 5:17 – "If anyone is in Christ, he is a new creation; old things have passed away; behold, all things have become new."

✅ Through Jesus, you are not just forgiven—you are made new.

Final Thoughts: The Gift of Forgiveness in Jesus

📖 Isaiah 53:5 – "But He was pierced for our transgressions, He was crushed for our iniquities; the punishment that brought us peace was on Him, and by His wounds we are healed."

Jesus paid the highest price so that we could experience complete forgiveness. Because of His love, we are:

- Freed from sin's penalty (*Romans 6:23*).
- Healed from guilt and shame (*Psalm 103:12*).
- Promised eternal life (*John 10:28*).

📖 Revelation 1:5 – "To Him who loves us and has freed us from our sins by His blood."

✅ Jesus' forgiveness is not just about removing sin—it is about restoring our relationship with God.

🙏 **Will you receive His forgiveness today?**

Chapter 11:
Forgiveness and
Reconciliation

📖 2 Corinthians 5:18-19 – "God has given us the ministry of reconciliation: that God was reconciling the world to Himself in Christ, not counting people's sins against them. And He has committed to us the message of reconciliation."

Forgiveness and reconciliation are closely connected, but they are not always the same thing. Forgiveness is a personal decision to release bitterness and resentment, while reconciliation requires mutual restoration of trust and relationship.

Many people struggle with the idea that forgiveness does not always lead to reconciliation. While God desires reconciliation in relationships, He also understands the importance of wisdom and boundaries when reconciliation is not safe or possible.

In this chapter, we will explore:

- Can you forgive without reconciling?
- When should reconciliation be pursued?
- Biblical example: Paul, Mark, and Barnabas (Acts 15:36-41).
- How reconciliation is possible when both hearts are transformed.

By understanding biblical **forgiveness and reconciliation**, we can learn how to navigate **broken relationships** in a way that honors **God, ourselves, and others.**

1. Can You Forgive Without Reconciling?

📖 Romans 12:18 – "If it is possible, as far as it depends on you, live at peace with everyone."

Forgiveness vs. Reconciliation

Forgiveness is unilateral—it can be given without the other person's participation. Reconciliation is bilateral—it requires the willingness of both parties to restore the relationship.

1. **Forgiveness is commanded**

o   Jesus calls us to forgive **everyone**, even those who have deeply hurt us.

o   Forgiveness is about **freeing yourself from bitterness** rather than excusing the wrong done to you.

2. **Reconciliation is conditional**

o   Reconciliation is possible only when **both parties** are willing to work through their issues.

o   It requires **repentance, trust-building, and a willingness to change**.

📖 Matthew 18:21-22 – "Then Peter came to Jesus and asked, 'Lord, how many times shall I forgive my brother or sister who sins against me? Up to seven times?' Jesus answered, 'I tell you, not seven times, but seventy-seven times.'"

✓ Jesus teaches that we must forgive continually, but He does not require us to stay in toxic or harmful relationships.

Biblical Examples of Forgiveness Without Immediate Reconciliation

1. **Joseph and His Brothers (Genesis 50:15-21)**

o   Joseph forgave his brothers **long before he reunited with them**.

o   He tested their hearts before **fully reconciling with them**.

o   **Lesson**: Forgiveness does not mean instantly restoring trust—it is wise to wait for true repentance.

2. **David and King Saul (1 Samuel 24:1-22)**

o   David had multiple opportunities to kill Saul, but he **chose to forgive** instead.

o   However, David did not reconcile with Saul because Saul remained dangerous.

o   **Lesson**: It is possible to **forgive and still maintain necessary distance**.

📖 Proverbs 4:23 – "Above all else, guard your heart, for everything you do flows from it."

✔ Forgiveness is an act of obedience, but reconciliation must be pursued with wisdom.

2. When Should Reconciliation Be Pursued?

📖 Luke 17:3-4 – "If your brother or sister sins against you, rebuke them; and if they repent, forgive them."

Steps Toward Biblical Reconciliation

Reconciliation is not just about forgiving, but also about restoring trust. It requires:

1. **Genuine Repentance**

o The person who **wronged you must acknowledge their actions**.

o There should be **visible changes in behavior** (*Matthew 3:8*).

2. **Willingness to Heal**

o Both parties must be **open to honest communication**.

o There must be a **desire for peace** rather than revenge (*Colossians 3:13*).

3. **Accountability and Boundaries**

o **Trust is rebuilt over time**, not instantly restored.

o Setting **healthy boundaries** prevents repeated harm.

📖 **Amos 3:3** – "Can two walk together, except they be agreed?"

✓ **Reconciliation should be pursued when there is true repentance and a commitment to rebuild trust.**

3. Biblical Example: Paul, Mark, and Barnabas

📖 **Acts 15:36-41** – Paul and Barnabas disagreed sharply over Mark and parted ways.

1. A Relationship Broken

• Paul and Barnabas were **ministry partners**.

- Barnabas wanted to take **John Mark** with them on their journey, but Paul refused because Mark had previously abandoned them (*Acts 13:13*).
- Their disagreement was **so intense that they separated**.

2. Time Brought Growth and Healing

- Over time, John Mark matured.
- Paul later recognized Mark's value in ministry (2 Timothy 4:11).

3. Reconciliation Happened When Both Hearts Were Ready

- Paul forgave Mark, but it took time for him to trust him again.
- Eventually, they worked together again in ministry.

📖 Colossians 4:10 – "Mark, the cousin of Barnabas, about whom you have received instructions—if he comes to you, welcome him."

✓ Reconciliation takes time, and God often works on hearts separately before restoring relationships.

4. When Reconciliation is Not Possible

📖 **Romans 16:17** – "I urge you, brothers and sisters, to watch out for those who cause divisions and put obstacles in your way that are contrary to the teaching you have learned. Keep away from them."

1. When There is Ongoing Toxicity or Abuse

- Reconciliation is not safe if a person continues in harmful or abusive behaviors.
- God calls us to peace, not to stay in harmful situations (1 Corinthians 7:15).

📖 Titus 3:10 – "Warn a divisive person once, and then warn them a second time. After that, have nothing to do with them."

✓ It is okay to forgive from a distance when someone remains toxic or refuses to change.

2. When There is No True Repentance

- If someone is not truly sorry or does not seek restoration, reconciliation cannot happen.
- Reconciliation requires mutual effort (Matthew 5:23-24).

📖 Proverbs 22:24-25 – "Do not make friends with a hot-tempered person, do not associate with one easily angered."

✓ Forgiveness is freely given, but reconciliation must be earned.

5. How Reconciliation Reflects Christ's Love

📖 Colossians 1:20 – "And through Him to reconcile all things to Himself, whether things on earth or things in heaven, by making peace through His blood, shed on the cross."

- God reconciled us to Himself through Jesus.
- True reconciliation reflects God's love and grace (Ephesians 2:16).
- Forgiving others demonstrates Christ's work in us (Matthew 5:9).

📖 Matthew 5:23-24 – "If you are offering your gift at the altar and there remember that your brother or sister has something against you, leave your gift there and first be reconciled."

✓ Reconciliation is a testimony of God's love to the world.

Final Thoughts: The Beauty of Forgiveness and Reconciliation

📖 **Psalm 133:1** – "How good and pleasant it is when God's people live together in unity!"

- Forgiveness is a command, but reconciliation is a process.
- Healing happens when both hearts are transformed.
- God is glorified when relationships are restored in His timing.

📖 Romans 5:10 – "For if, while we were God's enemies, we were reconciled to Him through the death of His Son, how much more, having been reconciled, shall we be saved through His life!"

✅ When we walk in forgiveness and reconciliation, we reflect God's heart to the world.

🙏 Will you allow God to heal and restore the broken relationships in your life?

Chapter 12:
The Eternal Reward of Forgiveness

📖 Revelation 5:8 – "The prayers of the saints are incense before God."

Forgiveness is not just an earthly principle—it has eternal consequences. God does not see forgiveness as an option but as a requirement for those who seek to live with Him forever. Forgiveness prepares us for eternity, aligns us with God's mercy, and influences the rewards believers will receive in heaven.

In this chapter, we will explore:

- How forgiveness prepares us for eternity.
- The judgment seat of Christ and the measure of mercy.
- Biblical example: Cornelius' prayers and alms brought salvation (Acts 10:1-4).
- How choosing forgiveness aligns us with heaven's standard.

Forgiveness is a reflection of God's nature and a key to eternal rewards in His presence.

1. Forgiveness Prepares Us for Eternity

📖 Matthew 6:14-15 – "For if you forgive other people when they sin against you, your heavenly Father will also forgive you. But if you do not forgive others, your Father will not forgive your sins."

Forgiveness is not just about our present relationships—it prepares our hearts for eternity. Unforgiveness creates barriers between us and God, hindering our spiritual growth and affecting our eternal destiny.

Forgiveness Ensures Our Relationship with God

- Unforgiveness hardens the heart and creates distance from God (Isaiah 59:2).
- Jesus emphasized forgiveness as a requirement for those who wish to receive God's mercy.
- Holding onto resentment is a spiritual burden that prevents us from entering into the fullness of God's kingdom.

🕮 Hebrews 12:14-15 – "Make every effort to live in peace with everyone and to be holy; without holiness no one will see the Lord. See to it that no one falls short of the grace of God and that no bitter root grows up to cause trouble and defile many."

✅ Bitterness can defile our spirit, making us unfit for God's presence.

The Parable of the Wedding Banquet

🕮 **Matthew 22:1-14** – "Many are invited, but few are chosen."

- Jesus described a great wedding feast (symbolizing heaven), where a guest was cast out for being improperly dressed.
- Unforgiveness is like wearing the wrong garment—it makes us unprepared for God's kingdom.

🕮 **Colossians 3:12-14** – *"Clothe yourselves with compassion, kindness, humility, gentleness and patience. Bear with each other* *and forgive one another if any of you has a grievance against someone."*

✓ Forgiveness is the proper garment that prepares us for eternity.

2. The Judgment Seat of Christ and the Measure of Mercy

📖 2 Corinthians 5:10 – "For we must all appear before the judgment seat of Christ, so that each of us may receive what is due us for the things done while in the body, whether good or bad."

The Bible teaches that every believer will stand before Christ's judgment seat to give an account of their faithfulness, obedience, and mercy.

God Judges Us by the Measure of Mercy We Show

📖 Luke 6:37-38 – "Forgive, and you will be forgiven. Give, and it will be given to you. For with the measure you use, it will be measured to you."

- God measures His mercy toward us by how we treat others.
- If we refuse to forgive, we limit the mercy that we receive from God.

The Parable of the Unforgiving Servant

📖 **Matthew 18:21-35** – "Shouldn't you have had mercy on your fellow servant just as I had on you?"

- Jesus told the story of a man who was forgiven a great debt but refused to forgive a small debt owed to him.
- The king in the parable rescinded his forgiveness and imprisoned the servant.
- Lesson: Forgiveness is a condition of receiving mercy.

📖 James 2:13 – "Because judgment without mercy will be shown to anyone who has not been merciful. Mercy triumphs over judgment."

✓ The way we forgive others will determine how God judges us.

3. Biblical Example: Cornelius' Prayers and Alms Brought Salvation

📖 Acts 10:1-4 – "Cornelius stared at him in fear. 'What is it, Lord?' he asked. The angel answered, 'Your prayers and gifts to the poor have come up as a memorial offering before God.'"

Cornelius was a Roman centurion who feared God, gave generously, and prayed faithfully. His acts of mercy and forgiveness positioned him for God's blessing and salvation.

Why Was Cornelius' Life So Powerful?

- He practiced kindness and mercy toward others.
- He had a heart free of resentment and bitterness.
- His prayers were heard because his heart was pure.

📖 Psalm 66:18 – "If I had cherished sin in my heart, the Lord would not have listened."

✓ A forgiving heart opens the door to answered prayers and eternal rewards.

4. Choosing Forgiveness Aligns Us with Heaven's Standard

📖 Revelation 5:8 – "The prayers of the saints are incense before God."

Forgiveness is worship. When we choose to forgive, our prayers become a sweet-smelling offering before the throne of God.

Forgiveness Prepares Us to Reign with Christ

📖 Revelation 22:14 – "Blessed are those who wash their robes, that they may have the right to the tree of life and may go through the gates into the city."

- Forgiveness keeps our robes clean before God.
- Only those who have forgiven others will enter God's kingdom.

📖 Matthew 5:7 – "Blessed are the merciful, for they will be shown mercy."

✅ **God rewards those who walk in forgiveness.**

5. The Eternal Rewards of a Forgiving Heart

1. Access to God's Presence

📖 Psalm 24:3-4 – "Who may ascend the mountain of the Lord? Who may stand in His holy place? The one who has clean hands and a pure heart."

- Forgiveness purifies the heart and allows us to draw near to God.

2. The Joy of a Heart at Peace

📖 Philippians 4:7 – "And the peace of God, which surpasses all understanding, will guard your hearts and your minds in Christ Jesus."

- Forgiveness removes inner turmoil and brings supernatural peace.

3. A Testimony That Glorifies God

📖 John 13:35 – "By this everyone will know that you are My disciples, if you love one another."

• Forgiveness is a powerful testimony of God's love.

4. A Place in the New Heaven and Earth

📖 Revelation 21:4 – "He will wipe every tear from their eyes. There will be no more death, mourning, crying, or pain."

• Forgiveness prepares us for a future without pain or sorrow.

✓ Choosing forgiveness aligns us with God's eternal purpose and rewards.

Final Thoughts: Will You Choose to Forgive?

📖 Luke 23:34 – "Father, forgive them, for they do not know what they do."

Forgiveness is not just about this life—it is a preparation for eternity. Heaven moves when we forgive because forgiveness reflects God's own heart.

📖 Matthew 25:21 – "Well done, good and faithful servant! Enter into the joy of your Lord."

✓ Will you choose to forgive so you can hear these words one day?

Final Words: Why You Must Forgive

📖 Matthew 18:21-22 – "Lord, how often shall my brother sin against me, and I forgive him? Up to seven times?" Jesus said, "Not seven times, but seventy times seven."

Forgiveness is not optional for believers—it is a command from God. It is not about excusing the wrong but about freeing yourself from the burden of bitterness, pain, and resentment. In this final chapter, we will explore:

- How forgiveness sets you free.
- Why forgiveness is the key to God's blessing and favor.
- How forgiving others makes you a true reflection of Jesus.

Many believers struggle to forgive, but the Bible makes it clear: forgiveness is the foundation of our relationship with God. When we refuse to forgive, we block our own blessings, hinder our prayers, and allow bitterness to consume our hearts.

This chapter will serve as a final encouragement to fully embrace biblical forgiveness so that you can walk in freedom, joy, and divine favor.

1. Forgiveness Sets You Free

📖 John 8:36 – "So if the Son sets you free, you will be free indeed."

Many people believe that forgiveness is for the other person, but in reality, forgiveness sets YOU free. When you refuse to forgive, you carry the weight of pain and offense in your heart. This burden affects:

- **Your mental health** – Bitterness causes stress, anxiety, and depression.
- **Your spiritual growth** – Unforgiveness creates **a barrier** between you and God (*Isaiah 59:2*).
- **Your physical health** – Studies show that **unforgiveness weakens the immune system** and leads to high blood pressure.

📖 **Proverbs 17:22** – "A joyful heart is good medicine, but a crushed spirit dries up the bones."

✅ **Forgiveness is a choice that brings healing to your body, mind, and spirit.**

The Weight of Unforgiveness

Unforgiveness is like carrying a heavy chain around your heart. Every time you think about what was done to you, it drags you down. But when you forgive, you break the chain and step into freedom.

📖 Hebrews 12:1 – *"Let us throw off everything that hinders and the sin that so easily entangles, and let us run with perseverance the race marked out for us."*

✅ Forgiveness removes the weight that slows you down in your spiritual walk.

Biblical Example: Paul and Barnabas

📖 Acts 15:36-41 – Paul and Barnabas disagreed over Mark, and their conflict led them to part ways. However, later in life, Paul forgave Mark and called him useful for ministry (2 Timothy 4:11).

✅ If Paul had stayed bitter, he would have missed out on an important relationship.

2. Forgiveness is the Key to God's Blessing and Favor

📖 Mark 11:25 – "And whenever you stand praying, forgive, if you have anything against anyone, so that your Father in heaven may also forgive you your trespasses."

Forgiveness is directly tied to God's favor in your life. When you forgive, you:

- Remove spiritual barriers that block blessings.
- Align yourself with God's mercy.
- Unlock doors that were closed because of bitterness.

Unforgiveness Blocks Your Prayers

📖 Isaiah 59:2 – "Your iniquities have separated you from your God; your sins have hidden His face from you, so that He will not hear."

If you are holding onto unforgiveness, your prayers may be hindered. God calls us to release others, just as He released us.

📖 Matthew 5:23-24 – "If you are offering your gift at the altar and there remember that your brother or sister has something against you, leave your gift there before the altar and go. First be reconciled to your brother, and then come and offer your gift."

✅ Forgiveness is a key that unlocks breakthrough in your life.

Biblical Example: Job's Restoration

📖 Job 42:10 – "After Job prayed for his friends, the Lord restored his fortunes and gave him twice as much as before."

✔ Job's breakthrough only came after he forgave those who hurt him.

📖 Luke 6:37-38 – "Forgive, and you will be forgiven. Give, and it will be given to you—a good measure, pressed down, shaken together, and running over."

✔ God's blessing follows those who forgive.

3. When You Forgive, You Reflect Jesus

📖 Ephesians 4:32 – "Be kind and compassionate to one another, forgiving each other, just as in Christ God forgave you."

Forgiveness is not just something we do for others—it is a way we reflect Christ to the world.

Jesus is the Ultimate Example of Forgiveness

📖 Luke 23:34 – "Father, forgive them, for they do not know what they do."

Even while hanging on the cross, Jesus forgave the very people who crucified Him. If Jesus could forgive:

- The soldiers who beat Him,
- The people who mocked Him,
- The friends who abandoned Him,

Then surely, we can forgive those who have wronged us.

📖 Romans 5:8 – "While we were still sinners, Christ died for us."

✔ True forgiveness is unconditional.

Biblical Example: The Thief on the Cross

📖 Luke 23:39-43 – One thief mocked Jesus, but the other repented. Jesus responded, *"Today, you will be with Me in paradise."*

✔ Jesus forgave instantly—no delay.

4. Are You Holding Onto Unforgiveness?

📖 2 Corinthians 2:10-11 – "Anyone you forgive, I also forgive… lest Satan should take advantage of us."

Unforgiveness gives the enemy power over your life.

Signs You Need to Forgive

- You feel bitterness when you think about a certain person.
- You avoid people because of past wounds.
- You replay hurtful situations over and over in your mind.

📖 James 3:14-16 – "If you harbor bitter envy and selfish ambition in your hearts, do not boast about it… For where you have envy and selfish ambition, there you find disorder and every evil practice."

✔ Unforgiveness invites spiritual chaos.

5. Let This Book Guide You into Complete Freedom and Healing

📖 Galatians 5:1 – "It is for freedom that Christ has set us free."

The choice is yours: Will you continue carrying the weight of bitterness, or will you choose to be free?

Steps to Walk in Forgiveness Today

1. Ask God to reveal any unforgiveness in your heart. (*Psalm 139:23-24*)
2. Pray for those who have hurt you. (*Luke 6:27-28*)
3. Release them completely into God's hands. (*Romans 12:19*)
4. Speak blessings over their life. (*Matthew 5:44*)

📖 Colossians 3:13 – "Forgive as the Lord forgave you."

✅ Forgiveness is a journey, but God will give you the strength to walk in freedom.

Final Encouragement: Choose Freedom Today

📖 Matthew 6:12 – "Forgive us our debts, as we also forgive our debtors."

Your eternal reward is tied to how you forgive. Don't wait. Let go. Be free.

📖 2 Timothy 4:7 – "I have fought the good fight, I have finished the race, I have kept the faith."

✅ Live your life with no bitterness—only love, joy, and the peace of God.

www.ingramcontent.com/pod-product-compliance
Lightning Source LLC
LaVergne TN
LVHW052036080426
835513LV00018B/2347